Amazon AMS Advertising for Authors

A Step By Step Action Plan to Produce Killer Ads That Work with a $20 Budget!

Copyright Chris Stockton 2018

This book is available in e-Book at most online retailers.

The right of Chris Stockton to be identified as the author of this work has been asserted by him in accordance with the Copyright, Designs and Patents Act 1988.

All rights reserved. No part of this publication may be reproduced, stored in or introduced into a retrieval system, or transmitted, in any form, or by any means (electronic, mechanical, photocopying, recording or otherwise) without the prior written permission of the writer. Any person who does any unauthorized act in relation to this publication may be liable to criminal prosecution and civil claims for damages.

Thank you for respecting the hard work of this author.

WHO IS THIS BOOK AIMED AT?

If this is you then keep reading.

You have a first book, or maybe two. They are already on Amazon as e-books. You would like to see some growth in sales, you don't have a lot to spend on marketing and need to make every dollar count.

If this is you then this book is not for you.

Already running successful AMS campaigns, have several books on Amazon and are looking to tweak those campaigns to make them just that bit more profitable.

OKAY LET'S GET STARTED

In this short book I am going to get you set up on Amazon with a number of AMS campaigns. We are going to produce several campaigns because I believe you need a number of fishing lines out there to find the right hook to get the readers buying or downloading your book.

What we are aiming for are steady constant sales, when you look at your KDP dashboard you will see weekly peaks and troughs which represent reading trends. I tend to find that Friday night is poorer than a Sunday. If your book is enrolled in Kindle Unlimited then the bottom part of the chart shows the page reads. So with AMS we are looking to generate a modest, and yet profitable 3-8 sales a day. That might not sound a lot, but that is every day and this is a starting point which can be built upon.

HOW MUCH IS THIS GOING TO COST?

I get asked this question a lot, and the answer is that if you are not careful this could cost you a huge amount of money. Some of my early campaigns were so expensive and wasteful they cost me a small fortune. It was a steep and expensive learning curve and what I'm going to share with you in the next few pages will hopefully avoid what you can see below.

What planet was I on when I thought it was a good idea to spend $103.61 to get so few sales. Yes I got $41.86 in sales, and this was my first successful campaign. This was the first time I had actually bagged a sale on AMS and I kept pouring money at it thinking surely it will get better. Well I am afraid the answer is it won't. All it will do is put a couple of sales on your graph and empty your bank account.

The reasons why I kept on plugging away with this, and believe me I am not alone are because it was getting me sales. The impressions figure I thought was quite high, and I hoped that off the back of the advert if people were not actually buying it then perhaps they were downloading it and I would make all my money back on KNEP. Oh how wrong could I be! Basically I gave Amazon £103.61. It gets worse, I kept on repeating this and running more and more campaigns that just burnt the bucks and produced me little in return. Finally my AMS bill topped $500 and I thought enough is enough – sound familiar?

Also notice I did get $41.86 in sales, however this is the top line and not a royalty figure. So my books were getting 70% royalty so roughly of the $41.86 I got to keep a whopping $29.30 to go towards my Amazon bill. The cost per click was way to high and $0.52, and I tend to find when the cost goes up the campaigns just don't work.

Now not only was this not going to make me any money on Amazon it was also not getting me any sales. The only winner here was Amazon. So we are going to set your campaign up so that you will be the winner and get some real benefits from AMS.

YOUR BUDGET FOR THIS PROJECT IS GOING TO BE $20

That is going to be your budget for this advertising project. Just $20. And if $20 is too much, then you can start with just $10.

Now if you are thinking you would like to invest more than $20, well that is fine, but please, let's start small. Find you some results and exploit those and get your book selling on Amazon.

I've recently set up a campaign for an author on Amazon. Cost per click is nice and low at £0.11, it has earned, in sales $13.98 and that will give a royalty figure of £9.77, with a cost of $6.13. So a profit. The ACoS column, (actual cost of Sales) shows a percentage of 43.85%.

So these are the columns we need to be aware of, our cost per click, total cost, sales and Acos. Take a look at your AMS dashboard and you can see the columns you need to keep an eye on there.

Before you can start to use Amazon AMS make sure you have a credit card attached to your account so that the monthly billing can be paid.

To do this click on the payment settings tab on your AMS dashboard and this will take you to a page where you can add your card. All very straightforward stuff.

So you now know that this isn't going to cost you a small fortune, and you have total control over your spend. You also know that you are not going to end up with stupid run away spend campaigns like I did. So let's get to the main event and start advertising shall we.

WHAT TYPE OF CAMPAIGN SHOULD I RUN?

You have a couple of options. These are sponsored products and product display. Because we are starting with a small pile of dollars we are going to run the first campaign using sponsored products. So you click on the New Campaign tab and then you will see some options, select sponsored products.

I've written a separate book on AMS product display ads, but for now, let's just keep everything simple.

These are keyword targeted adverts. This means that you can either ask Amazon to pick what it thinks are relevant keywords

OR you can pick some yourself. For advert one we'll let Amazon choose the keywords. Make sure your daily budget is $2, make sure your cost per click is set at 10c. These little insurance policies will make sure the campaign does not run away with itself. Should you find yourself distracted for a few days and unable to check into Amazon, it will have burnt the maximum of $2 dollars a day.

That said, I do want you to check into Amazon every day, this is so important to make sure this kind of campaign works. I shall explain why later.

NOW YOU NEED TO WRITE A KILLER HOOK FOR YOUR BOOK

Come on you are a writer - you can do this. There is a tendency to rush this and that is a fatal mistake. This is the advert that Amazon is going to serve up for your book, you have just 150 characters to write copy that is going to get people to your book page. Daunting isn't it.

Well don't panic there is help available. It's all over Amazon and easy to find in the form of other people's adverts. So if you write non-fiction books on How to Buy A House, type that in, click on one of the book results scroll down and you will see a host of books in the sponsored products section with their hooks beneath the book image.

Take your time, read through them, if there are some you like make a note. You are looking for something snappy, something that will scratch the itch the customer has and get him to click your advert. And I want you to do that ten times. We are looking to produce a series of 10 AMS adverts, so you need to write 10 compelling and different adverts.

I can hear you groaning from here. But just ask yourself how long did it take to write your book? Exactly, a lot longer than it will take to craft ten hook lines.

So get a notebook out, think about keywords and get writing.

LAUNCH YOUR FIRST FIVE CAMPAIGNS WITH AUTOMATIC TARGETING

So take your first five hook lines, and using the automatic targeting we have talked about above go ahead and create the campaigns. Yay, well done you are on your way. The slightly annoying part here is it takes Amazon a while to approve your campaigns so you'll need to check back in before you see any results.

MANUAL TARGETING KEYWORDS

So now we need to go ahead and create your first campaign with manual targeting, it is exactly the same as the above process (remember budgets and cost per click) just click on manual targeting.

Now Amazon is going to give you a host of "suggested keywords" and you can go ahead and click any on here and add them that you think are relevant. You can have up to one thousand keywords - yes that's quite a lot - and I can hear another groan.

So where to get yourself a big fat list of relevant keywords? Well it is a little time consuming, but that said, it's going to be worth it.

Open yourself up a spreadsheet and I am sure you can think of at least twenty relevant keywords straight away. Then if you follow this step by step guide you will end up with quite a list.

1. You can also add in to your list the name of other authors who write books closely related to yours. So make a list and add them to your spreadsheet. You can find these in two ways. Firstly should you write Highland Romances simply type that into the Amazon search bar and up will pop a lot of results, you can use the titles of these books as search terms and also the author names. Secondly go to your own book page and scroll down the to section customers who bought this also bought. Here you will see a lot of books your customers are also buying, and there is a tight link between your book and these others - so add the titles and the author names to your list.

2. Keywords and search terms. Lots of people get this wrong, and it really is worth just taking a minute to get this right. Sticking with the highland theme for a moment, type highland into Amazon and follow it with the letter 'A' - Amazon will provide a dropdown of what it thinks might be helpful results.

Not all of these might be relevant to our book, but Highland Adventure series might be along with highland avenger so we can add these to the list. Now you keep these going and the next search would be Highland 'B'. These are only examples, but try them out and you will see how this process can generate keywords.

Again not all the keywords might be relevant but we can grab a few and add them to our spreadsheet. Also note that you can refine this even further by typing Highland 'BA', and Amazon will serve up even more results, work through the options alphabetically – 'BE,' 'BI', 'BL' etc.

Get really creative, and don't tie yourself to one keyword. For example use Romance, Scottish, Alpha Male as your starting keywords. You will be surprised how quickly that spreadsheet starts to fill up. The method is exactly the same for non-fiction.

Be aware that there are a few banned keywords, for example Kindle and Amazon, and also you can't have special characters in your keywords either - (so no brackets) for example.

Now you have your spreadsheet done you can copy paste that into the Amazon keyword box. Sort out any issues Amazon does not like and you are pretty much ready to go.

I want you to use the same keywords from this spreadsheet to produce five manually targeted campaigns, each one will be different in that it will have one of your killer hook lines attached to it.

Now you have done all of this I am afraid you just have to sit back and wait until all your campaigns are up and running. It takes a couple of days usually, sometimes quite a bit less.

YOUR ADVERTISING STRATEGY

So all your campaigns are running, that's great news. So we need to monitor them and make some adjustments. It very much depends on what kind of book you are advertising as to how long your ads take to gain some traction. We are bidding a small amount so if this is a hugely popular area then it's going to take longer to get impressions.

Just as an aside, make a note of your Amazon ranking before you launch your AMS campaigns as this can be another way to judge the effectiveness of the campaigns.

This is really important, if you don't want to end up like me, paying loads of my hard earned money to Amazon for nothing. Keep an eye on your campaigns, if one of them reached $2 without a sale - kill it. Even it if has had a load of impressions do not be tempted to keep it running. There is a pause button and you can pause them or end them at anytime. The reason that the advert did not get any clicks is the hook line did not get them to the page (at this stage it could also be the cover but we will talk about that later).

So just keep those campaigns that are getting clicks and sales. And even when they get to 50% Acos kill them off.

This is all a learning curve. Campaigns that got impressions but not clicks are telling you something about your hook line.

ADVERT DIAGNOSTICS

IMPRESSIONS BUT NO CLICKS - Either your Hook line or your cover, or possibly both are letting you down. At this point the potential reader had not even seen your book product page so we know this isn't a cause of lack of sales.

IMPRESSIONS + CLICKS + NO SALES - Okay great work your hook line has brought them in but when they got there they didn't like what they saw and navigated away. Ask yourself if the keywords you used were relevant. If someone wanted a regency romance did you use that keyword and then when they got to your page they found they were faced with a teen vampire novel. That's an extreme example, but try and think like the shopper. If this was a manually targeted campaign you can look at the keywords that got impressions and clicks, just double check them for relevance.

IMPRESSIONS + CLICKS + NO SALES - If they have clicked then the likelihood is that it's not your cover that's put them off. They got to see this as part of the advert and the image, coupled with your hook enticed them to your book page. So is your book page letting you down? Have you written a compelling book description, filled in your author page, are you short of reviews?

IMPRESSIONS + CLICKS + SALES. Good job. This is really great, you've got a hook line that is working for you so develop it. Use it to craft some new hooks that are similar and when you've killed off a campaign that was just not working for you and had reached the $2 max start a new one.

If you get to the end of your $20 experiment and generated nothing then it's time to look at

Cover design
Book Description

If your advert and hook got them to the page ask yourself why did they not buy. What can I do to make my page and cover better. Stop advertising at this point and go into review mode.

Take a long hard look at your cover, then look at the best sellers in your category. The old adage is do not just a book by the cover, however all the buyer has to go on at this stage of the purchase process is the thumbnail picture of your cover and your hook. Think relevance? Does the picture provide a visual representation of what the reader will find between the covers? Does the picture "fit" with the keywords your book is appearing for? Have you fallen into the fiverr trap? There are some good cover designers there and some fairly poor ones. It's not the end of the world you can always revise your cover. I've run facebook polls before and asked my friends to choose between half a dozen pictures and see what they like and what they don't like.

Remember your cover appears as a tiny postage stamp sized image. Ask yourself – can you read your title? Does it stand out? Is your name on the cover too bag? Often authors make their names far too prominent, and this is off putting to the readers. They don't know who you are, and probably don't care yet. The title is the key at this point and the image on the front cover.

In particular if you book is non-fiction look at other best sellers, often there is a "fashion" trend in book covers. Make sure that your book fits in with the current style of cover. It makes it look more professional, up to date and helps you rank alongside other best sellers.

Have a look at my other book on how to refine your product page and see if you can make your description more tempting to the reader. Then you can re-run the campaigns that got clicks but no sales and see if the fix has worked. Your AMS results can tell you a lot about what readers are thinking when they see your page. Think relevance, make it tempting. A lot can be learned from looking at best seller product pages.

I am sure you have read this time and time again, make sure your author page is completed. Link it to your blog and website if you have one. Include a picture of yourself so that the reader can connect better with the author.

Check in at Amazon author central, make sure your books are included here. At the time of writing there is a different author central for Amazon.co.uk which needs to be set up separately from the .com version.

FINALLY

I hope you $20 campaigns work for you, keep the ones that work, constantly work on your hook lines. Let refine, refine, refine be your motto.

Look Out for my Other Amazon Guides

Amazon Book Product Page – Write a killer book page that gets sales – By Chris Stockton.

Ebook Cover Critique – Is your book cover letting your down? – By Chris Stockton.

Amazon AMS Adverts for Authors – Write Killer Product Display Ads with a $20 budget – By Chris Stockton.

www.ingramcontent.com/pod-product-compliance
Lightning Source LLC
Chambersburg PA
CBHW030111230526
45471CB00003B/1363